Standing in the Gap

Standing in the Gap

by

Aaron Espy

Cover Photo by Mike Meadows

1st Books-rev. 3/21/00

What they're saying

"Through his poetry, Aaron Espy expresses all of our feelings about the fire service. I have used his poems at memorial services, retirements, and during keynote addresses to inspire young men and women to become firefighters." *Chief Mike Brown, Kitsap County F.D. #7, Vice President, International Association of Fire Chiefs*

"Espy's poems are much like a high pressure hoseline armed with a smoothbore tip-powerful and penetrating. His ability to capture a firefighter's physical strength, courage and uncompromising compassion will make any firefighter's chest swell with pride and at the same time dampen many eyes." *Capt. Jim Perry, LAFD retired; Editor, **Los Angeles Firefighter***

"As a bereaved parent, Aaron's work is like music to my ears. His willingness to share his innermost thoughts as a first responder is a tremendous comfort to so many parents during the worst possible tragedy." *Joanne Cacciatore, Director, Arizona SIDS Alliance; Founder of the Mission for Infant Survival and Stillbirth (MISS); Author of **Dear Cheyenne***

"It is rare when a person who is not a bereaved parent can deeply touch the hearts of those who are. Aaron has that special talent-a very special ability-which few have, to use his words to touch the depths of a person's inner being and emotions." *Wayne Loder, Editor, We Need Not Walk Alone, quarterly magazine of **The Compassionate Friends***

Introduction

Few in our society today are quick to connect the words "poetry" and "firefighting". They seem as ill-paired as "church" and "tavern," or "pristine" and "polluted". Within the fire service, we prefer to propagate the steel-strong, muscley-macho image we've earned over the centuries. Poetry hardly seems compatible with that visual picture.

And yet, in some obscure closet in virtually every fire department across the continent, there hides at least one firehouse poet. A firefighter compelled to pour creative feeling about his or her profession onto paper.

Fearing the unmerciful teasing we firefighters are so famous for inflicting upon each other, most firehouse poetry writers prefer to remain closet poets, as opposed to the alternative of being "outed." There they stay, sharing their firehouse songs with neither peers nor public. Most go to their grave with this secret, and only when families sort through personal belongings is their poetry discovered.

Knowing full well that I will be the recipient of such ribbing, this poet comes out of the closet. Why? First, because I believe this genre of poetry is a part of our profession worth sharing. Secondly, I hope this collection will inspire other firehouse poets to step forward with their unique perspectives.

We can acknowledge this colorful aspect of our profession and still remain America's bravest. We can retain our reputation for valor and sacrifice not a scintilla of macho image. The public we defend has a right to see this side of us- to know we are mortal; hear our hurts, feel our fears and, on occasion, see us cry. Our humanity makes us no less rugged, no less courageous. It simply makes us real.

Aaron Espy

Dedication

When a firefighter lays life down, a community mourns. A region grieves. At times, an entire nation pauses to acknowledge. But time heals. Weeks pass, and community life returns to normal. The pain affects our fire department family much more profoundly. No one suffers more intensely, more chronically, though, than the parents of a fallen firefighter. While a fallen firefighter's extended fire service family may suffer for years afterward, the pain of the fallen firefighter's parents is measured in decades and lifetimes.

Those who changed diapers, laughed at a toddler's first tottering steps, waved goodbye to a kindergarten bus, cried tears of pride at a high school graduation; for them, life is forever changed. There will never be a "getting back to normal" for bereaved parents.

Standing in the Gap is dedicated to these who have lost the most, paid the most, yet are most easily and quickly forgotten. It is dedicated to the mothers and fathers of fallen firefighters everywhere.

Table of Contents

Chapter 1- Rookies

Chapter 2- Stethoscopes and IVs

Chapter 3- Engaging the Dragon

Chapter 4- In Defense of a Child

Chapter 5- Life in the Firehouse

Chapter 6- Unpinning the Badge

Chapter 7- Last Alarm

Chapter 8- Behind the Mask

Chapter 9- The Firehouse Poet

Chapter 1

Rookies

*Every seasoned firefighter has been **there**. Your heart pounds hard enough to rattle your ribcage. Saliva flees your mouth as quickly as a spilled glass of water disappears into mid-August Mojave sand.*

"There" is that first time you step into bunker boots, wiggle under suspenders, fasten your bunker coat and strap on your helmet in a "this is the real thing," life-and-death fire setting. "There" is that first time your whining red engine rounds a corner, bringing you face to face with a two story house belching black smoke and vomiting sheets of malignant orange flame. "There" is that moment every firefighter was born for, the challenge every firefighter dreams of. Every seasoned firefighter remembers being "there" for the first time.

It is a coming of age, this baptism of fire. A slice of time during which rookies demonstrate to themselves, their peers and their officers whether or not they have what it takes to stand in the gap.

"You Had to Be There"

What phrase does one use
to describe a telephone
that turns to liquid
and dribbles across
a smoldering countertop
like molasses?

Or the sensation that pounds
in the throat and temples
of a rookie when his engine
rounds a corner to confront
the red-orange glow
of his first fire?

What words do justice
to boiling black mushroom clouds
that pulse from the structure
he prepares to enter?

What sentence captures his delight
when he has found the source,
dispatched the demon,
and emerges from a potential tomb
to claim victory?

"You had to be there" comes to mind.

First Fire

Not much action, been real slow,
par for "C" shift rookies, ya know.
Nothing hot 'cept dumpster fires,
nothin' yet that singed my ears.

Alarm bell shatters my concentration
on the topic of cavitation
Tones pour through the station speaker-
"Engine 8, a structure fire."
This one sounds like its a burner,
Cap says it'll be my learner,
bunkers on and helmet tight,
hopin' I remember right,
B/A's on without a hitch,
as we roll I wait and watch.

Cap yells o'er the siren wails
that this one's garnered several calls.
He says, no, it's not surprising
down the 'ave to see smoke rising.
Closer now, I see it clearly,
split tri-level, it's a beauty-
Smoke from eaves and vents is rolling,
heavy flame one room's involving.
Heart is pounding down below
my tonsils (but just barely so),
praying that I'll come off looking
like I'm not a snot-nosed rookie.

His hand firmly on my back,
the Captain yells "a preconnect!"
He turns, and then shouts one thing more-
"I'll meet you at the friggin' door!"

I offer up a prayer of thanks
for hose extended without kinks,
for rocks that didn't send me falling,
shrubs that didn't trip me, sprawling.
Ready, at the door I stand,
Captain meets me, axe in hand.
Crouching low, my vision's poor-
push and turn, we force the door.

Up the stairway, this is different;
the training tower had no carpet!
Neither did I find this there,
(as I discard a teddy bear).

Captain's really pushing me.
Does he realize I can't see?
With each step the heat is building,
sure my helmet shield is melting.
Finally now, the flames I see,
heat has forced me off my knees.
Midway through my first real test
I hug the carpet with my chest.

Rolling orange and angry red
sea of fire above my head,
I raise the bail and reach for it,
but the Captain screams, "Not yet!
Three feet more, then open up.
You're sure to get a quicker stop."

Now, at last! I'm in position.
Aim and fire my Task Force stallion.
Water turns to hissing steam,
banking down like boiling rain.
Captain shoves me from the rear,
says, "We're not finished yet in here."
Crawling through a bedroom door,

snuffing tongues of stubborn fire,

as we move we make our search,
under beds and bookshelves reach,
while Engine Seven's crew of four
is searching both the rooms next door.

Cap and I are through at last,
E-Four's here, we've been replaced.
Down the hall and down eight stairs,
out the door, I breathe fresh air.
Tank and air mask hit the deck,
bet I lost five pounds in sweat.
As I drop down to one knee,
I can see Cap eyeing me
approvingly, as if to say,
"ya didn't do too bad today."
The Batt Chief from Battalion Two
asks, "how'd this rung-out rookie do?"
Cap just smiles, he looks real proud,
and says, " I think we'll keep this kid around."

Academy Blues

Say what?
Sorry, musta nodded off-
prob'ly somthin' to do with packin'
2 1/2" bundles to the top of the tower
all day long.

This is a ladder, this is a wrench,
here is a bowline- no, that's a clove hitch.
Boots could be mirrors they're so blasted bright,
polished so often I'm sick of their sight.

Run in formation, march in a row,
this is one step above boot camp, ya know.
Day after day, my head's crammed with facts-
Rope breaking strengths, the width of an axe.
Bust it all day, then study all night,
pray'n nonstop that my answers are right.

Why am I here, do I want it that bad?
I keep thinking of cushier jobs I have had.
But it's more than a job, it's a personal test-
I'm here till the finish, and so I'm just
try'n to survive until they disperse us,
into the ranks of the city's fire service.

Because it Matters

His parents wished for him
a more prestigious call,
complete with framed degrees
to hang upon his wall.
He chose, instead,
what beckoned him
since merry-go-rounds
and teeter-totters,
stolen away
by a siren song,
echoing loud, crying long.

Today he spends his waking hours
taking vitals, lifting stretchers,
turning couplings,
turning hydrants,
turning out to face the furnace.

Drawn to danger,
schooled by sweat
in his endeavor, asked why
he sacrificed a convertible
Lexus and tenth floor office
for flame-melted aluminum
and blood-soaked gauze,
he simply answers
"because-it matters."

Chapter 2

Stethoscopes and IVs

Emergency medicine: A term synonymous with the fire service. The golden-haired five year old struck by the car she didn't see; the silver-bearded grandfather who suddenly suffers from a crushing pain in his chest; the full term mother-to-be, stuck in rush hour traffic when her water breaks and contractions start. These are the victims firefighters stand ready to rescue. These, the patients who can't wait for treatment until they're safely inside the sterile, stable confines of a hospital.

I am Not Johnny Gage

Saves looked so easy during those
episodes of Emergency when a
Hollywood actor in a baby blue shirt
reached into black, frozen space
to retrieve a cardiac arrest
from a certain funeral service.

Johnny never lost a victim when I,
a fourteen year old wannabe,
sat cross-legged on the floor and
gaped at his heroism and his sly,
sideways smile that melted gawking
ER nurses into little white puddles of
opaque stockings and nursing caps.

Johnny's patients never vomited.
Watching him manage clean airways
did not prepare me for those smells,
gurgles and all that is least pleasant
about a human body in distress.

Nor did I learn from him how to tell
a wife of 32 years that there would be
no 33rd. I never saw him miss an I.V.,
or watch his patient slip off a cot
because a green EMT, panicked and trembling,
had failed to fasten a gurney strap securely.

Johnny never taught me Murphy's law.
But he was my hero,
and I forgave him years ago
for his deception.

Defibrillator

Funny how you
attract so many nicknames.
Innocent-looking little box,
you pick 'em up
just like Pigpen sucks up grime
in the Peanuts strip.

Bug zapper, sparker, juicer,
poor man's electric chair-
You are more misunderstood
than any equipment I carry
over a neatly manicured lawn and
into an otherwise quiet suburban
Victorian, now chaotic with
fear and the acrid smell
of grandpa's slip from consciousness.

They don't understand
how you restore life
by stopping it,
injure to heal,
hurt to help.
You are a riot control officer
bringing order-a
sea captain who
crushes mutiny
with a hum, a shock,
and a convulsing jerk.

Without you, I am no more
than a coroner pronouncing the obvious
on lifeless cardiac cells.

Quiet Killer, Silent Valor

You watch their attack
in amazement-
these men in fire gear
and breathing tanks-
as they advance into a building
that seethes with black smoke
and flame.
You shake your head in wonder
and think to yourself
what courage, what bravery,
(what stupidity).

But they lay life
on the line,
not only in the fire,
but every hour
of every day-

When they treat a bleeding
man with hepatitis-a coughing
woman with tuberculosis-an
accident victim bloodied, trapped
in a mangled car, who happens
to carry the AIDS virus.

Their bravery in the sick man's office,
the afflicted woman's home, is not
as apparent, as dramatic as on the fireground
where the car tires melt and paint blisters.
Yet in each, they show their valor-
every day,
every hour.

Friday Night

His girlfriend's scream is a duet with incoming sirens,
I cannot tell them apart at times.
Both echo in my head like a heavy metal song
in the cedar-strained moonlight.

Cool darkness is heavy with musty dampness
of sod suddenly torn,
as antifreeze and oil dribble from
an engine compartment, now accordion shaped,
its pistons heaved through the dash
to rest astraddle an Alice-in-Chains CD
and a coffee cup holder
still clutching a broken Budweiser.

Foggy, stale beer breaths
jaggedly come and go.
He doesn't talk to me,
only stares through sky blue eyes
that will not see tomorrow.

Twisted into space not big enough for both of us,
I race against his taker,
frustrated with him for leaving us
so little to work with.

Despite the mask and green-bottled gas,
his failing lungs collect less
than when I first arrived,
a cruel hoax on struggling intercostal muscle,
already oxygen deprived.

No brachial pulse now, just a weak carotid.
Suction, stabilize, needlestick to match the fourteen gauge
fired into his other limp arm,

yet all the while I know the outcome.

I forget to notice he is so young,
force from my thoughts the photo albums
stacked on his mother's coffeetable,
and his father's dreams of grandchildren.

Do we have an E.T.A. on airlift?
We'll take him out the left rear door,
the right side is blocked by that alder.

Disregard.
Cancel airlift.
We're gonna need a chaplain
and the coroner.

Overconfident?

Bold and cocky,
brash
on the surface.
Too often observed as
too sure
of ourselves.
But when hell
breaks and life slips,
who wants a
wimp?

Carried high
and proud,
because anything
less
would spawn
bacteria
of doubt,
patients
and their families
never see
our twisted
pains of

inadequacy.

Paramedics and ER Nurses

Professions so different,
yet so much the same-
they fight the same fight,
play the same game.
See the same patients,
feel the same fears,
shock the same cardiacs,
dry the same tears.

Splint up the fractures,
ice down the bruises,
one stops the hemorrhage-
the other transfuses.
One fights for life
on suburbia's floors,
the other duels death
behind glass trauma doors.

One fights the fire,
the other treats croup-
both taste the grief
on their mission to help.
Both of them serving,
both of them giving,
treating their patients
and always believing
their presence is vital
when someone's in need-
Divergent vocations,
similar breeds.

I'll remember you
(a tribute to medivac helicopter crews)

When I hear a chopper blade slice
the night air, as it drums
across the Puget Sound sky,
When it boldly roars out
of the cloud-covered night, landing
lights blinding my eyes;
When it settles in softly on our
landing zone, when the whine
of its engine slowly winds down, when
a crew in blue jumpsuits meets
this frazzled medic who is only
too grateful to see them-when
I look in their eyes for a
second of time, and glimpse
their compassion as
fervent as mine,
I'll remember your hands,
so skillful and sure,
that bagged my patient for me,
while a second gloved pair
of confident hands
traced a vein for a second I.V.
I'll remember your voices,
relaxed and upbeat,
as we spoke about our patient's care-
Encouraging, heartening, easing the tension
in a purely professional air.
But what I'll recall, more than anything else,
when I see a chopper in flight,
are the nurses and pilot who risked everything
to give hope to my patient that night.

Chapter 3

Engaging the Dragon

It gave our profession its name, yet with every passing year we firefighters fight less fire. We are more likely to stop an allergic reaction with a shot of adrenaline, shock a quivering heart back into rhythm, or dam up an ammonia leak escaping from an overturned tanker. Though it comprises less than 5% of what we spend our time doing, firefighting remains the most visible, the most dramatic, and arguably the most dangerous task we tackle.

We are not individuals eager to see our neighborhoods burn. We teach. We inspect. We train and practice, all in an effort to stop the next fire dead in its tracks. Yet every firefighter must admit that deep inside is a burning desire to confront the flames; to reduce the raging dragon to a sputtering, steaming, toothless wonder. No, firefighters don't wish ill on their neighbors, but if you ask an honest one, he'll tell you: "If it is going to happen- if it has to happen- let it happen on my shift".

Fireground

There is a place
where color does not matter,
where beliefs are not important
to anyone except the believer,
where male or female,
rich or disadvantaged,
makes not a particle of difference.

There is a place
where all that matters
is whether you are smart enough
to know the fire
is about to explode around you,
confident enough
to stand your ground,
wise enough to retreat,
strong enough
to pull your attack line
around yet another corner,
or brave enough
to push ten feet deeper
to save a life you do not know.

It is a place
called the fireground,
and like fire itself, it refines
and purifies, melds divergent
peoples and personalities,
convictions and biases, into
parts of a whole focused toward
a common purpose.

It is a place
where the bond of brotherhood

is better learned and lived
than in any other setting,
except that of war.

It is a place,
an experience
more people should encounter,
if we would ever learn
to live together.

Firefighters

Standing in the gap, these,
of courage and honor,
who place themselves
between the fire and its prey.
They give themselves to defend
life and livelihood
of those they do not know,
protecting what is cherished.
Their combat is all too often in vain,
yet still they confront
this relentless, merciless enemy.
They garrison our streets,
keeping vigil over our cities and burgs,
day by day,
waging a never-ending battle
against a nemesis who would strike
in a thousand different places.
They claim no distinguishing features
from legions of others,
save their unselfishness
and depth of commitment
to those they share life with.
They are professional firefighters, who,
for their great sacrifice,
ask no more than the respect
of those they serve.

Careless Butt

In this hot and sullen dead place,
it burps and passes its smoldered,
bitter gas;
In the black space,
full of silence,
save for the crackle of oxygen-starved flame,
we hear ourselves pant,
while sweat rivulets trickle
where we cannot scratch,
and our words leak through masks
as though strained by a mouthful
of cotton.

Over there, yes there!
Chest against cutpile carpet
we track its wheeze like hounds,
around one corner more,
and there, a glow,
an evil spirit
taken residence
in what once was a sofa.
Is this all?
It could have been
a better fight
for our trouble.

Out of Air

Ripping down ceiling, taking up slack,
working to finish the knockdown in back.
Alarm bell's been ringing for two minutes now,
just one more pull and we'll finally be through.

Breathing is tougher, my tank's going dry,
(this isn't a terribly good spot to die).
Shouldn't have stayed here this long, (don't I know it),
anxious and worried but _____ if I'll show it.

Hitting the stairwell, I'm almost back home,
I can see daylight but air is all gone.
Off with my mask and I'm down several rungs,
acrid haze burning my eyes, nose and lungs.

Gasping for breath, I complete my retreat-
never knew big city air could taste sweet.
Coughing and hacking, I'm blowing my nose,
embarrassed I cut it so stupidly close.

Swallow Hard and Go

Wisp of fear,
fleetingly pondered,
finds itself
tossed rudely into a corner
with other
semi-useless clutter.

Unwelcome Houseguest

Where she does not belong
is where she hides.

Predictable, greedy,
a terror and a coward.
Treacherous, savagely hungry,

she knows no reason or truce,
happiest when she foists herself
upon a helpless innocent.

She is a bully of the street,
and understands only
brute force of those

who stake their ground
and will not yield to her raging.

Part of the Whole

Defending a city they're paid to protect,
their strobe-flashing carriage rolls out of the bay.
Street signs, the light of the beacons reflect
as screaming, the bright engine gets underway.

Collars securing, their gloves they pull tight,
their redhatted officer scanning the sky,
opticom pulsing its lazer-like light,
motorists yield as the pumper flies by.

Through the rig windows they spot an orange glow,
adrenaline rushes are starting to churn,
engineer's airhorn a deafening blow,
rolling the four-lane they round one more turn.

Just past Pacific, a sharp right on Northrup,
voice on the radio curiously calm,
first due in engine is giving a size-up-
"Fully involved, strike a second alarm."

Lieutenant is barking, "let's lay a reverse!"
His crew is in motion before the rig stops.
Moving like gearwheels, they all intermesh,
quick and efficient without wasted steps.

Into the fury, they meld as a team
with others, opposing the furious blast,
taking their place in the system they form
into one body to finish the task.

'Til well past midnight the hot battle rages,
flame silhouettes hold a ghostly allure.
Fighting a war that repeats through the ages-
simplest of all conflict: water and fire.

Stairway to Conflict

Soles on the platform,
Stihl in his hand,
he stands-
From safety he parts
as upward he starts,
foot on the rungs
into a
sea of gold and orange.
Burning through early,
the flames are nearly
sweeping away
his resting place.
Perched like an icon
he works from the aerial,
not yet willing to
give her a burial,
cutting away
hidden years of
decay,
he's doing his part,
and hoping his work
will lessen the beating
his comrades are taking.

Reluctant Interview

When they're noticed publicly,
they blush and stammer awkwardly,

uneasy in the glaring lights,
content to wage less public fights.

It's enough for them, they say,
just to save one life today,

tap one fire before it spreads,
pull one victim from death's edge.

Confronted by the media mob,
they'll simply say, "just did my job".

Slaying the Dragon

Her tongue licks out
the front door, windows
explode
in response to her passion.
We attack
on elbows and knees,
suck dirt and scrape bellies,
inch underneath.
Beneath her
private underside
we aim a burst, brace,
and wait
as she
hisses and writhes,
raining down steam tears.
Cooler now, but
only barely-
advance, advance,
we take it back
from Jezebel,
queen of flame.

Incident Commander's Insomnia

A solitary form, he stoops among the carnage,
sifts the soggy, still-warm ash,
kicks twisted, discolored steel-
remnants of this battleground
that claimed a brother's life.
An acrid taste of blame
hangs in his throat,
like the hint of sulfur that
rides the fireground air.
If only he had seen...
if only he had called...
if only quicker to react...
if only... if only.

When an exhausted sun is chased by
flickering stars, with only a
bedroom ceiling as his witness
he will crucify himself more
gruesomely than any reporter could.
"You did your best,"
"you're only human,"
and all the other well meant
but empty consolations of
those who were not there
ease his misery no more
than water-fog from a hand line
vaporized by a five-alarm wall of fire.

If he's fortunate, turbulent sleep will
swallow him sometime between
two and three-a brief reprieve
from the ceaseless echo-if only.

Chapter 4

In Defense of a Child

Tough-guy image notwithstanding, a firefighter's stomach is twisted into a tight, muscle-spasming knot when a child is critically sick or injured. Never is the urgency more profound, the intensity torqued higher, the adrenaline thicker in a firefighter's veins than when a child's life hangs by a thread.

When the victim is a little person, firefighters burrow faster into smoke-choked apartments, crawl further into overturned cars, and dive deeper into murky water. The cry of a child pushes a firefighter beyond everyday limits to perform at levels that are, at times, almost superhuman.

First Child

The swamp, we call it.
The place where firemen go to cry.
Fifteen seconds from firehouse doors
at a sprint, yet safely out of earshot.
Its muddy-edged brown water,
home for too few trout,
too many pollywogs,
and a marriage bed for mosquitoes.

He was handsome, but green,
a foreigner to the marsh,
brimming with plans
to save his patients,
and in the heroic process
catch pounding female hearts
that fall into cupped hands
like soft, purple plums
from overloaded branches.

I shared the swamp with him
the sweat-soaked August night
he lost his innocence
to a head-on accident -
to a hazel-eyed child
not yet able to spell his name
or pedal without training wheels.

Two hours post-coroner,
he stooped above the equipment sink
to rinse tragedy from a rescue mask,
over and over,
as if water could splash
away the horror.
From across the truckbay,

I watched him,

his eyes fixed somewhere
just above the water
that circled, then chased itself
down the drain.

From somewhere inside came
"I think it's clean enough, John.
Lets walk."

In the heavy summer stillness
we trampled ferns and crumpled swampgrass
'til we stopped at water's edge.
I left him there,
half kneeling, half squatting
beside a half rotten maple log.

With a shirtsleeve I rubbed a circle
on the dust-caked window of yesterday
to see myself
cradle a tiny, lifeless form,
swallow the boulder
in my throat for the fourth time,
and pray I would not break
before I was alone.

I left him there, in fading light,
his pain muffled by cricket song
and a merciful wind
to rustle the alder leaves.

Ask Me

Ask me what I like about this job.
I'll point to that little boy
with the Buhner-Buzz haircut
hip-hopping down the baked July sidewalk.

He jumps from one square to another,
balancing on one foot,
then the other,
arms aflail,
doing everything within his power
to stay off those dreaded cracks.

He pauses when he catches sight of me.

He doesn't know me.
We've never talked before.
But I'm a fireman,
and that propels me to a level
just below the sweat-streaked,
hammer-wielding construction framer
he calls "daddy."

Ask me what I like about this job,
and I'll show you that little boy
who loves me
just because I drive a twenty ton Pierce
with razor-red and white-hot lights
that burn through crisp night air.

Little Firefighter

Always in her dreams at night,
and sometimes in her days,
she drives the shiny engine
with its flashing lights ablaze.

Sitting high behind the wheel
her wide eyes brightly glow,
as in her mind she navigates
the diesel down the road.

The fire she fights is fantasy,
alarms an apparition,
yet even now it beckons her,
this noble aspiration.

But she must wait impatiently;
time moves too slow, it seems-
So for today she'll be content
to dream her firefighter dreams.

Sleepless Nights

I walk my backyard border
at half past three,
Nikes soaked from grass
hung heavy with dew.
Embarrassed to cry,
afraid to curse,
I confide in the stars
that pulse through Puget mist.

Her blue emerald eyes,
her tiny hands that wore
a plastic Barbie bracelet
and cradled a purple teddy bear-
forced from my mind
as I fought against time-
they tear at me now,
too drained to fight,
too restless to sleep.

After too many years,
After too many faces,
her eyes shadow me
as if this was the first time-
as if I'd never been
the first to say goodbye.

Thank you, God, that it was me
and not another who would
not have stroked her hair or
held her hand like I know
her father would have done
if he were riding with us.

Fair Trade

Pepsodent white,
his teeth were straighter
than Lincoln's memorial columns.
Certainly straighter than mine.
He flashed a condescending smile my way
when I told him what I did.

"There's not much money
in firefighting, is there?"

I smiled back through slightly
crooked teeth set in a face
not half as tanned, and fished
from my wallet, burdened with
dog-eared pictures and tattered
pay stubs (but precious little money)
a faded, grade school image
of a giggling girl who once lay
on the highway shoulder,
hair matted with blood,
pea gravel clinging to her cheek
as if she were a magnet
for roadway refuse.

"Her mother gave me this,
when they came to meet
the medics who brought her back,"
I told him. "Rhonda's her name."

Keep your Ferrari. I have her picture.
Thanks, but no, I'm not trading.

Pediatric Box

It's a regular
morning routine,
half-full java mug steaming
on the medic unit bench seat.
Ten-thousand-alarm-club veteran,
I open a cabinet door
to find the box there.

I breathe
a heavenward request
for any other crisis
than one to force release
of these three latches,
drawing urgent fingers
toward a hollow tube,
one tiny, silver-bladed scope,
and razor-peaked needles
in plastic sheaths.

Reliving every reach
for a slipping child,
I pray,
"give me an adult in need,
but spare me vacant eyes,
and mottled hands
that will never cradle matchbox cars,
fresh dandelions,
or circle daddy's finger."

In Defense of a Child

Though hot the flame and thick the smoke,
though swift may be the river,
he steels himself against the tide-
he is a firefighter.
Whether at a child's bedside,
in the street, or fire-
Though the desperate fight for life
be in the frigid water-
No matter where the battleground,
or what the circumstance,
he plays the hand that he's been dealt
to steal this child a chance.
Whenever fate would dare to rob
a child of precious breath,
whenever cruelty would snatch
a little one in death,
no matter who or what the cause
of life-or-death encounter,
between a child and hopelessness
there stands a firefighter.

Chapter 5

Life in the Firehouse

When firefighters aren't responding to a 911 call, we're likely to be busy at our second residence- the stationhouse. The firehouse is our home for 24 hours at a time- nearly a third of our lives. It's there that we eat, sleep, keep ourselves physically fit, and forge lifelong bonds almost as strong as those of flesh and blood.

In more ways than not, we are like any other family in any other home. We laugh, play, argue, and, like any other family, when the heat is on, we close ranks and protect each other's hindquarters. Hang around a fire station long enough, and you'll discover what makes a firefighter tick.

Coming On

On the road at O-six-thirty, turning left on Main,
one more dawn like any other, coffee tastes the same.

Down the onramp into traffic, I-5 is a mess.
At the station by seven-thirty, that would be my guess.

Sure enough, the training tower juts against gray sky,
just as I am pulling in at seven twenty-five.

Strolling past the hanging bunkers, no one need inquire-
by their pungence it's apparent- C shift had a fire.

In the bunkroom, boys are stirring, Luke's rubbing his back.
Doug is blinking, Mike's still sleeping, Jessie looks a wreck.

Sliding belt around a waist that's now size thirty-four,
(wasn't it a thirty-two just five short years before?)

Passing arms through navy sleeves, I wonder where time's gone.
Blurring shifts and seasons fade like finger-sifted sand.

What emergencies will try me through this twenty-four?
Who will live to see tomorrow, who will close life's door?

Just what challenges await me, where will be the fires?
Gunshots, fuel spills, crumpled cars,downed and arcing wires?

Shining boots and collar brass, I walk the tiled hall,
thinking just how blessed I am to answer duty's call.

One more day like any other? Never quite the same.
Each one different, each unique- a firehouse page of time.

Ode to George
(Rookie Engineer)

If you think you're gonna earn
the right to drive here, son,
there are a few things you must learn,
so list'n   t' how it's done.

When you sit down behind the wheel
of this big red machine,
and roll that eighteen tons of steel
called Engine Seventeen

down city streets and four lane highways
answering the call
of folks in trouble, don't forget
to make the siren wail.

Keep checkin' all your gauges, son,
and mind the intersections.
Make sure you know where you are bound,
don't stop t' ask directions.

Above all, son, remember this-
when you are underway,
you gotta drop a CD in
and crank up ol' George Strait.

This fire station has traditions,
things we've done for years;
Now one of them is George's music
and his country tears.

When danger calls and fire threatens,
George's music calms

our fears and worries, 'specially on
the third and fourth alarms.

His clear voice floats across the cab
and mingles with the wail
of siren song and blasting horn
reminding all is well.

A ballad or pure country gold,
it just don't really matter-
as long as good ol' George is singin'
we'll snuff any fire.

So just remember this, my boy,
when you charge out that gate-
Blow your siren, hit your lights,
and crank up ol' George Strait!

Firehouse Coffee

Created with such good intentions,
what evil has this become?
Bold and piping
when the day was fresh,
now bitter and biting-
like a romance gone sour,
with no easy way out.

Leftover Leftovers

Twice too often in the microwave,
dry as sand, too gone to save.
Looking at first like a chef's forte,
five alarms later, it's DOA.

Come and eat- no, never mind-
there's a vehicle fire at 3rd and Pine...
Now it's done- wait just a sec-
some guy on Spruce just wrenched his neck...

Finally, now, it's on the table.
IF you're willing, IF you're able.
Knife and fork, they just won't do-
get the Hurst, the chainsaw too.

Will you taste it, are you brave?
Is it easier, lives to save?
Such are meals for Cap and crew,
down at station forty-two.

Firehouse Hand

I wheel the Ford extend-a-cab into the parking lot,
and plant the F-250's tires in their usual spot.
My fingers grab the bag that holds my extra clothes to wear,
my toothbrush, comb, deodorant, my antique shaving gear.

While climbing down, I swing the bag up over my right shoulder.
The strap pulls snug against my neck, above my flannel collar.
I turn and pause to drink it in- the cragged, serrated range-
I never tire of the Rockies, never wish for change.

I picture early fires fought by valiant of the city-
no doubt, with simple bucket lines... it couldn't have been pretty.
I wonder how this country looked before the asphalt streets,
before the cars, the power poles, and well before the fleets

of fire trucks that fill the stations, sprinkled through the towns-
I think of how it must have felt to cinch a saddle down
before beginning morning's work of mending fences torn-
that was my grandpa's first real job before my dad was born.

My grand-dad rode a horse named Max beneath Missoula sky,
but my steel coach drinks diesel fuel, its barn a firehouse bay.
My mount does not require shoes, it has six wheels instead;
no longer chestnut brown, it gleams a candy-apple red.

My pistol is an Akron grip, my boots are rubber lined.
My rifle bartered for an axe, my rope no cattle binds.
And yet, despite the dunes of sand
 to trickle through time's 'glass,
I cherish those old cowboy ways,
 though ninety years have passed.

I live, like them, a simple life- my values are the same.
Our code of sweat-soaked, honest work
is timeless and unchanged.
My view of life is like a mirror, despite the passing years,
to early century hands who stoked the fire beneath the stars.

I hope if they could see me now, out here beside my Ford,
they'd tip a weather beaten brim with an approving nod.
Yes, there are still some noble ways for men to make a living-
the old cowboys of yesteryear are nowadays firefighting.

Best of Professions, Worst of Professions

Being a firefighter is the best job in the world when

- *Your outstretched fingers reach through the hot, black fog to find a salvageable child.*
- *You walk through the firehouse doors in the morning knowing you'll spend the day doing something that matters.*
- *Your friend says he's envious because you love your job.*
- *A grateful citizen says "thank you".*

Being a firefighter is the worst job in the world when

- *Your outstretched fingers reach through the hot, black fog to find a fellow firefighter's lifeless body.*
- *You walk through the firehouse doors on Christmas morning, knowing you will spend the day apart from the ones you love.*
- *Your doctor says he's sorry because you have job-related cancer.*
- *An under educated politician says you don't need a raise because you already make too much money.*

Bonnie
(Groundbreaker)

Blond and fair, solidly built,
she walked through the door
and announced herself.
Jaw set firmly,
determination reflected
in her aquablues,
confident but nervous,
not sure the pioneer image
really fit her. Still,
she was there,
and had resolved
to remain,
despite the smoke
and blood,
or the dubious scan
of her lieutenant.

Launched in her career
to prove nothing
to anyone, except herself-
On the line
for none other
than love of challenge
and reward of making a difference-
No longer seen
by those she sweats
and fights beside
as a novelty,
there is no lingering question
of respect-
for she has earned hers.

Oh Dark-thirty

Out of the dream-laden, echoing deep,
we stumble from fog-shrouded haze of our sleep,
pumping like divers up to the surface,
out of our cobwebs and into the harness.

Jolted awake by the bells that now call us,
list'ning intently and trying to focus,
process the dispatch with eyes still ablur,
ponder the questions of who, what and where.

Onto the engine but still not quite with it,
suspenders askew, hands in gloves hard as granite.
The Captain's impatience rings clear in his voice-
"Can't you move faster, is that too much to ask?"

Dispatchers wary and pensively nervous,
hearing no engine yet sign into service,
Cap's nasal twang finally rides the airwaves-
Engine eighteen is at last underway!

The Fight to Revive

Responding to a cry for help
we react instinctively.
Always in the middle of trouble,
the pressure heavy on our shoulders,
tension thick enough to taste,
arriving to find our worst fears
confirmed, the situation is bleak,
but yet we work.

The finest minds, the bravest hearts,
the right equipment for the job,
I watch my teammates kneeling, hovering,
laboring unselfishly to revive this white,
middle aged victim, without thought to
the smells, the mess, the unpleasantness,
for we were born for this.
Brian pumps in rhythm,
sweat beads drip from his forehead.
"Hold your compressions,"
I direct, as I check to see if
normal flow has returned.

We've walked this road before,
and I am never prouder than
when I work with them.
Our eyes meet, knowing from
experience the outcome may not be a good one.
Suddenly a shudder, a splash, and life returns.
We smile and exchange high fives.
This is one firehouse toilet
Roto-Rooter will not have to fix.

Old Engine 22

What stories you could tell
if brass and chrome
had voice-
Clanging bells and whistles,
steam from other time
and place.
Are you glad
you bowed out early
from technology's wild race?
If you could speak
what would you think
of counterparts today?
Are we better,
or just different-
just what would you say?

If God is Gracious

If fortune smiles,
if God is gracious,
we will not scatter a comrade's ashes
on the bitter mountain wind,
nor don white gloves and golden braid,
nor casket drape in patriot colors.

If God will smile,
and God be gracious
bells won't toll for yet another,
pipes won't cry for brothers lost.

Despite God's plan
or random fate,
white lights will flash,
twinsonics slash the clinging fog,
for these who answer each alarm
are not deterred by what may come,
and only pray
that they are not fate's terrible prize,
that God is smiling,
God is gracious,
that flags will ride their standards high,
and pipers will not have to play.

As pistons churn, and engines turn,
we pray God smiles on us today.

Union Prez

Alone, he slides the grievance papers
to their rightful place.
Halfway through another round,
he closes his briefcase.
He never grumbles, but his darkly
circled eyes reveal the strain.
His shoulders droop a little more-
though he will not complain.
He grapples with the how's and why's
of ten percent who do the work,
while ninety just slide by.
In vain he searches for the answer
to a question that still plagues-
Why are the folks the least involved
the quickest to complain?
He flicks the lights, and locks the door
to the silent hall at midnight's hour,
and as he drives, he justifies-
is this commitment worth the price?
He fights the urge to close his eyes,
and squints against oncoming lights,
as lost in weary thought, he drives
back to his home and loved ones lives.
He parks the car, unlocks the door,
then softly up the stairs he creeps
to wife and children, long asleep-
To a lonely family who has seen
too little of this man, this week...

Chapter 6

Unpinning the Badge

Every firefighter who survives thirty-odd years of fireground hazards must one day confront the bittersweet moment he leaves the service. He works his final shift, sits in the officer's seat of his engine one final time. Cleans out his locker. Says goodbye.

For every man or woman who passes through that experience, there is a sense of accomplishment intermingled with sadness, expectation married to remorse. There is satisfaction in reflection on a career of lives saved and fires stopped. There are mountaintop memories of death cheated and life lived on the edge, and a twinge of pain at leaving it all behind. You'll never hear a retiring firefighter say, "I'm sorry I chose that line of work."

Billy-Bob

He holds the little Maltese cross, insignia of the brave,
department token of esteem for twenty years he gave.
He rolls it over in his fingers, staring at the pin.
Beneath his oversized mustache there breaks a quarter grin.

He drifts back to an April day some twenty years ago
when first he pinned that silver badge on his blue uniform.
His hair, once fire-red and full,
is thinned with streaks of gray;
A little slimmer then, nowadays he sports a stockier frame.
Since 'seventy-five he's held the line
for neighbors and for strangers.
He's faced the flames and highway wrecks
with all their many dangers.

His gruff, no bull exterior in truth, is there to hide
the caring, soft, gigantic heart that's carried deep inside.
It shines through in the gentle way
 he holds the injured child,
his hand upon the shoulder of a victim at the fire.
Despite the pain and loss he's seen,
the suffering and the tears,
he's never, even once, regretted serving all those years.

His other loves pull hard upon the strings of his big heart;
his wife, his kids, his fishing boat
that sometimes just won't start.
Someday he'll bid a fond goodbye
to bunkers and suspenders.
His truck and boat will take him
where the fishing stream meanders.
But until then you'll find him waiting, ready when you call.
When you're in need, dial 9-1-1, and pray that you get Bill.

Measure of Success

When he looks back on his career
a fire officer does not weigh success
like others do.
He measures not
in hundreds of business deals made,
thousands of transactions closed,
or millions earned.
Though he may not leave his profession
renowned or wealthy,
in the mirror of tomorrow
his achievements will be reflected
in lives of subordinates
he has developed,
homes and businesses he has preserved,
and victims he has helped to save.

Heroes

We look for them,
jersey-clad,
to light the playing field
with moves we only dream about...
We search for them
behind the badge,
rescuers who face the flame
that lights the midnight sky
before they snuff it out...

But heroes visit quietly-
God puts them in our lives
to touch us with a gentle hand,
brighten gray sky
with a smile-

They teach us silently,
without a word sometimes,
in quiet strength they live their lives,

and if we search their memory,
we'll find what God would have us be,
a hero of the silent kind,
who leaves this world
a brighter place
than when we first arrived.

Men Like You

There are those
who make life's pathway
a perpetual quest for gain...
to acquire status, accumulate things,
erect self-monuments of fame.
And when they're gone,
they leave a world
no better for their journey,
no better for their name.

And then there are a special few
who walk the selfsame trail,
who never miss a chance give,
a fallen brother to assist,
a noble cause to serve.
They live out their conviction,
model purest passion,
teach us what is right,
and how to fight
for what is true.

Once in awhile
they walk the trail with us-
we've been blessed
to walk awhile
with you.

Chapter 7

Last Alarm

Firefighters work in dangerous environments fraught with deadly surprises. On the fireground, death crouches in fire-filled rooms and lurks beneath burned out floors. Medical scenes bring danger of another sort, killing an infected firefighter slowly, years after an exposure.

We know ours is a dangerous profession. We love life and love our families. We are not martyrs, so we make every available preparation, take every known precaution, to protect ourselves. Yet try though we might, the unexpected explodes when we are most vulnerable, and too often a firefighter pays the ultimate, surrenders that which is most valuable.

When a brother or sister dies in the line of duty, we go to great length to honor their sacrifice. It is our way. From the public we serve, we ask only that our fallen be remembered. Remembered for their courage, for their selflessness. And while their memory may fade with revolving seasons and rolling years, we ask that they never, never be forgotten.

Down the Runway

With the telephone's ring
my answering machine
breaks yet another tragedy.
"Can you come," they ask,
"to honor him
with your poems?"

In a handful of hours
a 737 rockets me down the runway,
headlong into leaden clouds
and sobs of valiant men
in formal dress blues,
wives in black veils,
and fatherless sons
who fidget with clip-on ties,
trying to be brave because
daddy would have wanted that.

Tomorrow I'll approach
the lectern
after a brother's eulogy,
before a pastor's prayer,
and wrestle with the lump
rising from my chest,
only to be lost,
between verses,
in the eyes of his wife, wondering
what were their last words,
how long their last touch?
My eyes will not meet his son's-
His eyes are fixed on the floor,
and I will wonder
if my little man would also find
a firefighter funeral

a bore.

I'll leave the church
and some will thank me.
Others will not notice
as they flounder in their grief.
A Hertz rental, another plane,
another terminal,
and I'll be home again
to kiss my wife,
squeeze my children,
and ponder why
the youngest and the bravest
must leave us
with such regularity.

The moonlight that seeps across
a decade's worth
of his valentine and anniversary cards
scattered across
her kitchen table
finds me standing at a kitchen window
half a continent away,
praying tomorrow's poems
are not read for me.

America Remembers

A gallant, noble sacrifice,
a priceless life laid down—
So rare the public servant's worth,
no greater treasure found.
No greater act of decency,
no greater human love—
No greater courage demonstrated
by the lives they gave.

This tribute to unselfish hearts
today will testify
that health and safety have a price—
that firefighters die.

The shadow of this sentinel
into tomorrow cast,
forever will the gravestones shield
of heroes who have passed.

It bathes their tombs in bravery,
and brands upon our memory
the gift they gave, the canceled debt,
let towns and peoples not forget
the price they paid to keep us safe,
our lives and homes secure.
We honor these who gave their all,
their memories here endure.

His Brother's Keeper
(In memory of Seattle firefighter James Brown: 1971-1995)

Cut from valor's fabric,
Tailor-made to bear
Another's pain,
Diamond 'mid the gravel,
Kind, unselfish, helpful,
Always giving
In a land preoccupied
With getting.

Unlike his brotherhood and family,
The world will miss him little.
As for so long
They did not miss
The gold
In Sutter's Creek,
The oil
In Texas clay,
The Rembrandt,
Dusty, forgotten, hidden
In the antique store
Downtown.

For those who grieve
January's loss
To a human race
Already too short
On goodness,
His smile glitters clearly
From His new station
East of that sunset,
North of those stars.

When You Remember Me

If I am ever called to leave you,
unexpectedly,
please take from me these parting thoughts
to frame my legacy.
When you remember me tomorrow,
I pray you'll recall
A happy soul who loved his family-
Loved his work as well.

Please recollect a man
who loved the chance to lend a hand,
to save a life or property
from some untimely end.
Someone who heard the public call
to safeguard streets and homes-
deliver breath to silent lungs,
to quench the hostile flames.

But when you ponder how I came
to make my final stand,
don't make me more than what I was-
a kind, compassionate man.
Don't make me more in death
than I, in life, have ever been-
Remember, simply, one who served
his God and fellow men.

I Travel Light

Dress blues,
jeans and sweatshirt,
Nikes and black wingtips-
An overnight bag that bulges
like grandpa's post-Thanksgiving stomach.
Of course there are my poems,
just as wrinkled
as the T-shirt and jockeys
they're sandwiched between.

There isn't much that's needed here
in this swollen-eyed
and tear-streaked town.
Just someone to help bury the dead
with more fitting words
than trite political phrases
from lips that have never tasted
sulfur, sweat and blood.

I smooth the pages,
re-read the lines,
long since memorized,
press them flat
and visualize
a thousand dress blue uniforms
with yet one more
who paints his poems upon their cheeks,
blending with their tears
and memories,
words to salve their grief.

Headed home
this time

they ride
near the Benadryl
and Motrin,
folded neatly once again
in a side compartment,
medicine for someone else's soul.

Duty's Call

When duty called,
He answered with his honor-
Like few others,
gave what he had and more.
Protected, we who slept,
gave scarce a thought's release
to what was giv'n,
we drifted off
in peace.

But those he loved,
and those who loved this man,
knew well the risk
that he might not return.
That in some hostile framework
he might fall,
who knew the price
might someday be a piper's call.

They lived with risk
that someday he might lay
'mid wreaths and flowers
in solemn reverency.
While these, our quiet tears
of pride run free,
because we loved him
unashamedly.

6 O'clock Headlines

One by one they alternate tragedies.
News anchor tongues
thump like a beaten drum.
I found you there,
limp, eyes vacant,
stuffed like sandwich meat
between the stale white bread
of a class action suit
and the weary tax feud in
congress -

A fireman dies.

Cropped tightly,
clips short and piercing
to save airtime,
dramatic enough to recapture
distracted stares,
your sacrifice measured only
by ratings impact.

Tomorrow shouldered lenses
and slack microphone cords
will chase a fresher story,
while a fresh grave cries
for a headstone not yet placed,
and a fatherless seven year old cries
alone.

There is news to cover.

Quiet Hero

A quiet kind of hero,
you never found your name
in lights, or on a marquee sign,
you never tasted fame.

You never signed an autograph
for one adoring fan,
or heard the roar
of thousands more
resounding from the stands.

You never wrote a novel,
never ran for public office.
You never were a TV star,
or occupied a palace.

Instead you found your destiny
upon the fireground stage,
where wars are fought for human souls,
where conflagrations rage.

You forfeited your chance for wealth,
laid down your chance for fame,
and chose instead to give your life
to ease another's pain.

No history book will tell your tale,
but this the world should know-
You died just as you lived.
You were a quiet kind of hero.

Half-mast Morning

Curled around a frozen aluminum pole,
left that way by a breeze that died
sometime last night, halfway up a
dull, gray shaft, that forlorn,
wilted flag. It hangs limp, like
yesterday's rose left thirsty,
forgotten, in the sun.

I don't have to ask why.
I don't want to hear that
somewhere in my family
a widow agonizes over which
dress to slip on, which one to wear
when she views his shell
at the funeral home, as she
wipes away the tears that
run down her little girl's cheeks
like water bubbling
from a park drinking fountain.

When I see that flag
I know what I hate most about this job.
More than ill-informed, opportunistic politicians,
more than twisted meth addicts
who poison themselves and lease out their children
to pedophiles.

I hate that half-mast flag because
I know this morning our world
will have one less who is willing
to leave so another can stay.

Yesterday, Tomorrow

Snows and summers will not blur
the smile that spread across his face.
The golden leaves will not impair,
nor April blooms that fill the air
his memory erase.

Though from the spotlight he may fade,
no correspondent breathes his name,
and should the town he served fall silent,
though he finds no lasting fame,
though disappearing trail the years
through mists of time and drying tears,

yet there will stand a place, a moment,
bold and proud above the fray,
where men and women will recall
his selfless acts of yesterday.

As seasons roll, like river current,
time will smooth away the pain
to heal our hearts, but not obscure
the life he did not live in vain.

To make a difference

From somewhere deep within,
from sometime long ago,
you made a promise to defend
a life you did not know.
You heard the call, you filled the need,
you served with strength and grace.
"To make a difference" was your creed,
for that's how you were raised.

Your choice was not the gentle road,
you could have trekked another-
you could have chased the flash of gold,
to serve yourself, not others.
Instead you chose this sacrifice,
a debt we can't repay,
our tears cannot renew your life,
or bring your smile back today.

The gift you gave, the price you paid
will never be forgotten,
as surely as your life you gave,
our gratitude is written;
Inscribed today on history's page
for all the world to see,
a lore of one who modeled courage,
a hero's legacy.

Lion Hearts

Born within these little boys,
planted long before they'd grown,
there beat a scarce, unusual gift,
long before their course was known.
It hurled them onto treacherous paths
where others could not, would not tread,
where other souls from peril shrank,
we found them standing in our stead.

Some say they loved the sirens,
were enamored with the danger,
still others say they craved the challenge
of a raging fire.
Or was it raw, unbridled valor
seeking but a chance
to shine its light for one brave hour
into a perilous circumstance?

Their gift, a seldom rivaled feat,
their hearts with lion courage beat,
through water deep or raging flame
they'd risk it all yet once again.
If you would understand their bravery,
taste their salt of valor,
watch their brothers fight for life-
for they were firefighters.

Unbroken Bond

Never a bond more fierce,
than one of pride and pain.
Never stirrings deeper pierce
than summoned by the bagpipe strain.

Never a pain more keen,
than loss of one who gives,
who counts the cost, their gift lays down,
so other souls might live.

Never a loss that deeper cuts,
yet drives our hearts together.
Never a soul we bid good bye,
yet lives with us forever.

Locker Door

He won't be coming back
to close his locker door-
this one right here with
the picture-cloaked interior.
An open locker door,
left carelessly ajar,
he left it just this way,
for it was just an average day;
Gone for just a moment,
on just another call,
another structure fire,
another siren wail.

Standing wide you see inside
the snapshots of his life-
A boy on a trike, his camping wife-
Here it stands ajar,
a shrine to what he was,
full of treasured memories, these,
the special frames he chose;
His bride in glamour pose,
and a birthday rhyme whose author
was his thirteen year old daughter.

And buried, hidden deep behind,
his only piece of shame-
a uniform long since too small
for his expanded frame.
If you look hard, strain through the tears,
you'll read in smiles and radiant eyes
the story of his checkered life,
for here the silent guardian angels
shield his memory, taped to his locker door,
the one he won't be back to close.

The Wall

They've come from every walk of life,
our continent's every corner-
We etch their names upon this wall,
in granite stone their lives we honor.
Each one, a different story tells of bitter tragedy,
of courage- written on this wall,
lives given for community.

The world won't long remember them
without this monument-
Our globe, awash in suffering,
where countless other lives are spent.
But in this honored, reverent place,
their memories brightly shine.
On this green field beneath the Rockies,
thankful hearts a tribute find.

When men and women ask the question,
"What do firefighters risk for me?"
These names of valor echo back,
"We've purchased your security
with precious offering of our lives,
with families torn by grief,
with selfless, sacrificial duty,
fervent our belief
that someone must defend the lives
and property of all-
Our pledge so fully did we keep
that now, we line this wall."

One Less Man of Honor

Another of our bravest dies,
another tragic price;
This world is so much poorer now,
because he lost his life.

This world has one less man of courage,
one less man of honor;
This world, that knows too few like him,
has one less man of valor.

Yet he lives on in each of us,
his strength with us remains.
He leaves his courage and his heart
with all who breathe his name.

Although we grieve his leaving,
although with tears we mourn,
he leaves this world a better place-
his smile lingers on.

Our Firehouse Prayer

Just maybe, this will be the year
we fly no flags half-mast.
No shrouded badges, funeral prayers,
memorial flowers or streaming tears;

Just maybe once, since long before
we ever started counting,
no firefighter would have to die,
no gift of gallant sacrifice,
no empty boots, no empty chair-

Just maybe, this will be the year
when all our family makes it home,
no casket draped,
no bagpipe drone;

Just maybe once, we'll honor those
we've lost in years gone by,
but add no more names to the wall,
for none have had to die.
So as we face another year,
Lord hear us in our fervent prayer-
protect us safely through the fire,
and maybe, this
will be the year.

Chapter 8

Behind the Mask

Few of us reveal our real selves to those we serve. Firefighters have a public image to uphold, a persona to perpetuate. We jealously cherish our reputation as heroes, as bulwarks of strength. Our grandfathers handed us this reputation, and we are proud to carry it.

But we are learning we can be real. We can cry with grieving families over the loss of their child, or wonder at our own mortality without sacrificing an ounce of our reputation for bravery and honor. We prove our courage every time we enter a structure where flames melt the aluminum out of window frames. We have nothing to prove to our citizens, yet old traditions die hard.

Captain Castwell's Getaway

The song in my ear twelve hours before morn
was the yelp of a siren, a bellow of horn.
Now the whoosh of my flyline floated over the eddy,
launched from the gravelly bar on this jetty
spawns a fresh music- a riverland chorus,
with scream of a bluejay and thunder of rapids.

These fingers now joining this tippet to fly,
just yesterday hoisted a bundle and wye,
while fire-gloved hands that yesterday raised
the thirty foot ladder and probed the thick haze,
find a gentler task stripping line, pulling slack
in fog-shrouded dawn on this overgrown creek.

Crystal water, clean air purge my lungs, heart and mind,
as the flame and the nozzle I leave far behind.
As my offering drifts into this rock-sheltered pool,
I wait and I watch, a flyfishing fool,
who just for a cherished few hours more,
is at peace on the water, away from the fire.

Prayer of a Fireman's Wife

Another day, another shift,
he's out the door again.
Lord guide his footsteps, hold him tightly,
safely in your hand.
He smiles and tells me not to worry,
yet I know so well,
there are so many circumstances
he cannot control.
Keep him secure as he responds
with engine lights ablaze.
Protect him on the battlefield
of fires he'll engage.
Preserve and guard this fireman,
Lord shield him from the flame,
and bring him back securely, safely,
home to us again.

Eye of the Beholder
(A tribute to foster parents)

Two firemen out for driver's training
drove the beach highway.
The younger said "I'll show you beauty like
you've never seen before today."
The younger drove the two-lane road
that skirted golden sand,
and pulled the engine to a stop
while pointing with his hand.

Between the highway and the surf,
below the summer sun,
four women lay in meager suits,
their quest a deeper tan.
"Have you ever," said he wryly,
"seen a sight more grand,
than all these slender, lovely ladies,
prone upon the sand?

Look at all these lovely ones
with curved, voluptuous frames.
Scant-i-ly clad goddesses,
with blowing, flowing manes
that sparkle in the midday sun,
and dance upon the breeze.
Tell me, now, where can you find one
lovelier than these?"

The elder's silver hair blew softly,
yielding to the wind.
The lines of wisdom on his face
broke in a weathered grin.
The old man answered not the question,
uttered not one word,

84

but gestured that they travel further
down the beachfront road.

As the younger drove,
the old man pointed out the way-
First left, then right, then straight ahead
until they'd left the bay.

They traveled to a modest street,
a modest neighborhood,
and parked beside a big gray house
with weathered, cracking wood.
"I've seen your beauty," said the wise one
as he looked around.
"Now let me show you where I've learned
real beauty to be found."

He straightened and his eyes grew bright
as through the door she came,
this woman in a dirty dress,
while 'round her children played.
The woman stood 'mid seven kids,
yet none of them her own-
this foster mom had weighed the cost,
had opened up her home.

Seven little children, in her arms
and clinging to each knee,
abused, neglected, tossed upon
life's cold and brutal sea.

Her body was not thin and lithe,
she carried extra pounds.
Her fingernails, from ceaseless work
were worn and broken down.
Her face was plain and streaked with sweat,
no makeup did she wear.

A faded cotton handkerchief
held up her plain brown hair.
Her pale blue eyes, though strained and tired,
were filled with peaceful grace,
as smiling, with her hand she wiped
ice cream from one child's face.

They watched the children, once abandoned,
lost- without a home,
as they swarmed her on the porch,
this woman- strong and calm.

The old man, turning to the younger,
said to him while smiling,
"do you find the beachfront, son,
to still be so beguiling?
Beauty's a subjective thing
to each and every eye.
It springs from deep within one's heart-
from values one lives by."

They left the quiet neighborhood
in silent, wordless drought.
The elder, ever quiet man,
the younger, lost in thought.

Beyond Boundaries

There is such a thing
as feeling too much of a patient's pain,
the melting of your soul
together with a parent who has lost a child,
a family who has lost a home,
or a suicidal man who has lost his family
and the will to live.

There is such a tragedy
as falling into their abyss,
the tearing of your soul's flesh
weeks, months, years after the crisis.

There is a place that harbors
only danger for your soul,
that envelops you in perpetual darkness,
daily depression, continual grieving.

There is a place that lies beyond
crying for a dying child,
a place beyond compassion,
a place into which no caregiver ventures
to return whole again.

There is a bottomless gulf that waits,
that gapes for those who cross the line,
for any who dare carry another's burden
beyond the boundaries.
It is bordered on the its opposite side
by hardened, shale and jaded cliffs
of indifference and unfeeling numbness.

There is such a place
that neither in your waking hours

nor in your dreams
must you ever venture,
a chasm into which you must never fall,
and yet you must walk its edges daily,
for it is there you fulfill your calling.

There is a narrow, treacherous path
over which a helping heart must walk-
It lies between the two extremes.

Badge of Faith
(A tribute to Chaplains)

Just beyond the searing flame,
beyond a broken body,
just above a siren wail
that echoes in the night,
at yet another tragedy
the man of faith serves quietly,
just because the hurting need him,
just because it's right.

He fights a vastly different foe
than those who face the fire,
his heartening word and gentle touch,
a tonic for the soul.
While others fight for life
the chaplain heeds a higher calling;
a human bridge to share God's love,
the wounded heart to heal.

Although he may not tame the blaze,
or aid an injured child's respire,
no matter when, no matter where,
you'll find a fire chaplain there
to dry the tear,
to ease the hurt
of a tearstained face,
and a broken heart.

Stream Of Tears
(A tribute to bereaved parents)

I try to imagine
what your grief is like,
and then you show me.

I imagine a storm,
you show me a hurricane.

I imagine a stream of tears,
you show me a flood.

I imagine emptiness,
you show me endless expanse
of the universe.

I tried to imagine,
but could not understand,
until you showed me.

If

Your love has given life to me,
revealed the rainbow's color;
where once before drab shades of gray
would darken daylight hour.

Before you smiled, I did not live,
I struggled to endure.
But now I see the reds, the blues,
of wine and sky, the yellow hues
of dandelions and rhododendrons,
these I never knew-

Before you came to light my world,
this love I learned from you.
And if I never see the glint
of golden morning sun,
if God should choose to call me home
before the coming dawn;
if I should never know the touch
of sprinkled April rain,
or breathe perfume of garden roses,
wet with dew again;
If wisdom far beyond our own
determines we must part,
do not forget, my dearest one,
this fire will burn though I am gone-

Its warmth through countless years the same,
and from its embers, light your flame.
Though I should leave,
my love remains.

Where I ride

Torn apart were we,
no time to say goodbye.
Tonight I bear my starlit gift
of peaceful sleep below,
shine through your bedroom window
on a pillow stained with tears.

Close your eyes and find me
in places where I used to be,
for this is where I ride

the early summer sunlight playing warm
upon your shoulders,
dance with December's snowflake,
soundless,
mingled with your hair,

skim the salty white-capped swell
on early April breezes,
rustle in the browns and golds
of crisp October air.

Let gently go of what I was
for I am so much more-
I am not with you as I was,
yet I am with you still.
And you will always find me
on springtime's April breezes,

where I ride the silver moonlight
soft into your dreams.

From Me, to You

Since you're gone this holiday,
I wonder what I'll give to you.
How I'll wrap a warm embrace,
a warmer smile you cannot see;
How to mark it so you'll know
that yours is the one with the emerald bow,
with blue and sterling wrap reflecting
twinkling lights that dance in circles
'round a fragrant, fresh cut tree.

Since you've gone I often walk
the starlit paths we used to stroll,
and there, among the ferns and cedar,
heavy with first winter snow,
I look into December nights,
and hope for your familiar shadow
in the silver moonlight glow.

Since you've gone I oft' remember
what you whispered in my ear.
Through the tears, I've learned to see
those sun-warmed days, just you and me;
Remembering all I loved the best;
Remembering, just the way you asked,
for I am learning, with your help,
to find the sun above the rain,
the 'bow of colors beyond the pain.

Since you're gone this festive season,
You will find my present here
In Puget-red Olympic sunsets,
golden dawns on frosted air,

high above the Cascade range
you'll find it framed in distant blue-

Since you're gone this holiday,
a poem will be my gift to you.

I wonder

Isn't that the same guy
who flipped us off yesterday
when we blocked traffic for the
baggy-panted Korean boy
lying bloody and still
in the street beside his skateboard?
I wonder, did we make him late?

I wonder what he thinks of us,
rubbernecking from his Saab convertible
as he drives home to a waterfront rambler sprawled
across the salty pea gravel of Alki Beach.

We, poor soot-covered fools,
who root through a collapsed skeleton
that used to be a Guatemalan family's dream-
we who chase camouflaged embers
that hide from our pick-headed axes
and curved closet hooks.

I wonder, is he content
at night in master suite darkness
as he stares at shadows
that play across his ceiling
from the headlights of distant cars
that melt into the Seattle blackness?
Does he think about us when he hears a siren
that crescendos, then dies just as gradually?

Does he wonder what we do when he's asleep?
When the siren wakes him at three,
midway through his predictable
eight hours of sheet time,

does he picture us thrusting latex-gloved fingers
into an open stab wound to dam up the spurting blood?
Or does he curse us for waking him?

I wonder if he is pleased with his life,
his stock splits
and sixty foot, double-masted sailing ship
moored at the yacht club.

I wonder if he knows
we scream at our children's football games,
make love on living room floors,
count quarters to see
if we can afford a ski trip to Banff.
Just like him, except maybe for the quarters.
I wonder- Is he happy with his life?

Trigger Points

I know a fireman who remembers,
 ... if he hears the screams of playing children,
 an occupied house belching flame
 and polymer-laden smoke.

 ... as he passes that scarred maple on the roadside,
 one willowy, dark-haired mom who left two toddlers.

 ... when his hands grip rough-cut cedar,
 the split-rail fenced farmhouse
 where he lost his first SIDS.

I am a fireman who remembers,
 when I hear the phrase
 "I don't want to be any trouble,"
 a charred, fingerless man,
 skin seared like leather,
 who touched me, eye to eye,
 his pleading for relief
 prefaced by that phrase.

 Our toxic memories,
 splashed like dirty engine oil
 on a white carpet floor,
 we are firemen who remember.

Daydreamer

After the engine is back to bed
in the bay, the axe is cleaned,
the tanks refilled, the report finished
and in the outbasket, he heaves a sigh
and lets go of his work,
lifted away to another place in time
where he can observe without her knowing.
Dark and flowing with a streak of gray,
tomboyish, but striking-
a real head-turner, confident in
whatever she challenges,
hiding it well when she isn't.

He sees her in a dozen different modes-
once on her knees in the garden,
wrist-deep in the dirt she loves,
then astride her chestnut,
white-blazed horse,
weaving between the boughs.

He watches soundlessly
from beyond her view, for if
she knew she would be self-conscious.
And the fact does not escape him
that she is more beautiful than
the painted females he meets
every day, without even trying to be.
He cranes for a better look as alarm
bells shatter his pleasure, and
she is gone like frost on a September morning.

"Engine 16, Cencom, responding."

Chapter 9

The Firehouse Poet

We are sprinkled through firehouses across our continent. Most departments have at least one. Despite our own self-doubt or the sideways glances of our peers, we are compelled to continue writing about the house fires, head-ons, and practical jokestry our comrades plague each other with. We write because we must. For those of us who pen firehouse poetry, the inclination runs in our fire-engine-red blood.

Addiction

Fingers, butt and toes
sprout roots into
keyboard, chair and floor.

Play with word puzzles,
round off edges,
sharpen others,
begging them fit together,
I frown before
my VGA mirror
that on occasion reflects
coherent thought.

More than my hobby,
my keel of sanity;
Some firefighters
hunt, mountain bike,
some cast dry flies,
still others
drink and play
divorce court.

I write.

Chosen Circle

'Round the room you're seated,
suffocating the table
with your knees and forearms.
Coolly you hold me at bay
with your credits and degrees.
Is there a place at your table for me?

Simple fireman, I look into your eyes
and fight your waves of intimidation
(or is that just my imagination?)

Verbs; verbs and proper pronouns,
dazzling adjectives and metered,
rhythmic stanzas are what you demand.

I swallow and manage to whisper
that all I have are these denim,
faded, Kevlar thoughts that seem
to rhyme more often than not,
and tears that splash down
firefighter faces, bathe American
flags in triangular cases.

Here I am
with my word collections,
patchwork of pain and bravery,
paper sentinels to guard the tombs
of those worth remembering-
With only my simple fireground songs,
is there a place at your table for me?

Blue-Collars Need Not Submit

..and we can't use anything but free verse.
Sorry, only previously published
need apply.

Your work needs spondee-nay-i-tee;
and where, exactly, is your meter?
(midway down our slushpile)
We know good poetry when we
smell it-
        yours, well...
        have you thought of
        a writer's conference?

We'll take your Visa,
and put you on our
mailing list
for just ten dollars more

        and what is it about
        firemen and
        their bleary-eyed wives

that makes them cry
when they read
your novice work?

Firehouse Poetry

It's not the least important
that the poet isn't polished,
or that the fireground song he writes
is only by him, cherished.

No matter if it rhymes or not,
and never mind its structure,
regardless of the grammar used
to paint the fireground picture,
what matters more than anything
above all else is this-

It formed within a fireman's heart,
the raging heat and flame he felt.
While purists seek perfection,
they'll lose a poignant lesson
in bravery and unselfishness.

A few will glimpse a noble art
the others surely miss-
Our poets from the firehouse,
in rhyme will show you this.

Extend a Helping Hand

Your purchase of this book supports the following charities:

1) **IAFF Burn Foundation.** The International Association of Firefighters Burn Foundation contributes to burn care and research by funding research grants and scholarships for burned children to attend burn camp.

2) **Northwest Burn Foundation.** This Pacific Northwest organization funds similar projects on a regional level in addition to providing counseling and monetary support for Northwest burn victims and their families.

3) **The Compassionate Friends.** TCF is an international bereavement support network with over 550 U.S. chapters. This organization provides emotional support to bereaved parents and siblings. It also provides educational material to professional groups who must deal with parents whose children die, such as hospitals, law enforcement agencies, and fire departments.

4) **IAFF Fallen Firefighter Memorial.** The IAFF FFM, located in Colorado Springs, Colorado, is a memorial to professional firefighters who have lost their lives in the line of duty. One of the author's poems, America Remembers, is inscribed at the base of one of the monuments at the memorial.

5) **National Fallen Firefighters Memorial.** This memorial, located in Emmitsburg, Maryland, honors all firefighters, career and volunteer, who have given their lives in the line of duty.

About The Author

Since 1978, Aaron Espy has served the citizens of the Pacific Northwest as a firefighter. Espy has written his firehouse poetry since first stepping into bunker boots, but kept his work private until the death of four Seattle firefighters in January, 1995. Since that time he has seen over 60 poems published in fire service newspapers, magazines, and newsletters. His poem, *America Remembers*, marks one of two monuments to fallen firefighters at the IAFF Memorial in Colorado Springs, Colorado.

Espy's work has also been published nationwide by grief support organizations including The Compassionate Friends and the Arizona SIDS Foundation. He has also contributed to multiple magazines as a freelancer, and has written a 911 column for the Scripps-Howard West Sound Sun. His work appears at a website titled *thefirehousepoet.com* . The site showcases this book and his other works, and also details upcoming appearances and future publications.

Espy currently serves as Assistant Chief of Training and Emergency Medical Services in Mason County, 20 miles Southwest of Seattle. He lives with his wife, Kate, and their two children, A.J. and Annie, in Southworth, Washington. His daughter Amanda, 20, lives in nearby Port Orchard.